D0886599

Song and Dance

BOOKS BY ALAN SHAPIRO

Poetry
After the Digging
The Courtesy
Happy Hour
Covenant
Mixed Company
Selected Poems, 1974–1996
The Dead Alive and Busy
Song and Dance

Prose
In Praise of the Impure:
Poetry and the Ethical Imagination
The Last Happy Occasion
Vigil

Translation
The Oresteia by Aeschylus

Song and Dance

Alan Shapiro

HOUGHTON MIFFLIN COMPANY

Boston   New York

2002

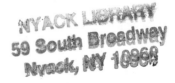

NYACK LIBRARY
59 South Broadway
Nyack, NY 10960

Copyright © 2002 by Alan Shapiro

All rights reserved

For information about permission to reproduce selections
from this book, write to Permissions, Houghton Mifflin Company,
215 Park Avenue South, New York, New York 10003.

Visit our Web site: www.houghtonmifflinbooks.com.

Library of Congress Cataloging-in-Publication Data
Shapiro, Alan, date.
Song and dance / Alan Shapiro.
p. cm.
ISBN 0-618-15285-7
I. Title.
PS3569.H338 s6 2002
811'.54—dc21   2001039527

Printed in the United States of America

CRW 10 9 8 7 6 5 4 3 2 1

Design by Melissa Lotfy
Typefaces: Granjon, Spectrum

Grateful acknowledgment is made to the following publications,
in which these poems originally appeared: *Greensboro Review:*
"The Match." *Pedestal:* "If I Only Knew Then," "The Old Man."
Slate: "Scan," "The Phone Call," "The Accident."
Threepenny Review: "Broadway Revival." *Tikkun:* "Joy."

This book was greatly aided by a fellowship from the
Project on Death in America of the Open Society Institute
and by a fellowship term at the University of North Carolina's
Institute for the Arts and Humanities.

For Ellen, Arana and Rachel
Angels of Mercy

In memory of
David Eric Shapiro

Contents

Everything the Traffic Will Allow   1

Transistor Radio   4

Sleet   8

Scan   10

The Match   17

The Phone Call   23

The Accident   25

Joy   28

Up Against   31

The Last Scene   33

Fly   37

The Big Screen   39

Three Questions   41

Broadway Revival   43

If I Only Knew Then   46

The Old Man   49

To the Body   50

Song and Dance   54

Last Impressions   57

Song and Dance

Everything the Traffic Will Allow

The two boys don't suspect
                    they don't exist.
And Ethel Merman is
                    the shade of a shade —
what Plato says
                    all poetry is —
                         a record
spinning beneath
               a needle
                    as the boys
lip-sync into
               imaginary mikes
her glottal swagger,
                    brassy, large,
                              streetwise
and from their mouths
                    so touchingly naive
for being so . . .
               There's no
                    people
                         like show
                              people . . .
Their parents clap
               and whistle
                    from the bed,
propped up
          on pillows . . .
                    Everything about

it is appealing . . .

             They are shouting "Encore!
Bravo!"

       when the boys,

           like chorus girls,

arms on each other's shoulders,

              step-kick their way

across the room

        and out of it,

           then back . . .

stealing that extra bow . . .

           Shades of a shade.

What poetry is.

       Because there's nowhere else

for them to be

      except

         inside the room

in which it isn't

       when it is,

          in which

there is no room

       unless I think of it —

the boys

     their arms flung wide

            on one knee

mouthing the last words

         before the needle slides

off into silence,
        the parents propped up
                on pillows,
half laughing, half
        shouting "Bravo!
              Encore!"
                  All now
just the shade
        of a shade —
             like no
              people
                I know . . .

Transistor Radio

Far down the beach
the roller coaster rippled in the heat haze

like a curvy bright
white trellis carved from cloud that a faint breeze

would scatter, though it held
somehow, somehow seemed more impalpable

for having held, for not
dispersing when the train of black cars

inched up the airy hill
of it to plunge down suddenly with a speed

that from far away looked slow
as reverie. How old was I? Free

for an hour from my weekend charge,
my traveling "companion" — my grandmother

alone at her rich brother's
beach house, with the shades drawn, the doors locked,

the bloated, stroke-crippled
indigent body hobbling from bed

to kitchen, kitchen to bed,
chain-smoking, muttering curses against her daughter,

her ex-husbands, against the cold
heart of a grandson who could just walk out

on her like that, too far
gone in her head to care about or notice

the trail of piss or shit
she left behind her always wherever she went,

which it was my job
to clean up. Why I was made to come. The beach

was beautiful with bodies,
far off among the lazy swells, or strolling

to and from the surf,
or lounging all around me on sides, backs, bellies,

like a vast lair
of languid animals, or young gods stretching

and turning over, rubbing
themselves or each other with creams and lotions

up and down already
gleaming arms and shoulders, calves and thighs.

Inside my head the shit
trail, the piss trail, the stench, the ceaseless muttering.

Outside me, though, salt air,
fragrant oils, and the ever-shifting zones

of tinny croonings that
got louder and softer at the same time

as I wandered out among them,
down the beach, away from her, my every stride

delivering a new song
or the same song, each one another letter

in my new alphabet
of feeling. *Somewhere beyond the sea, somewhere . . .*

They were all so beautiful,
the boys and girls. *Dream lover, until then . . .*

Their bodies sang themselves.
They sang, *Come softly, darling, come to me, stay.*

It was so easy to.
So easy to forget. To keep on walking.

Your little hand in mine . . .
The beach went on and on. There was no end

to it—*My heart was flying*—
the massive bright white trellis that no white

was ever whiter than —
the way it rippled in the heat and held

so airily together
when the cars plunged over and the boys stood up

in the free fall waving
while the girls beside them shrieked the whole way down.

Sleet

What was it like before the doctor got there?

Till then, we were in the back seat of the warm
dark bubble of the old Buick. We were where
we'd never not been, no matter where we were.

And when the doctor got there?

Everything outside was in a rage of wind and sleet,
we were children, brothers, safe in the back seat,
for once not fighting, just listening, watching the storm.

Weren't you afraid that something bad might happen?

Our father held the wheel with just two fingers
even though the car skidded and fishtailed
and the chains clanged raggedly over ice and asphalt.

Weren't you afraid at all?

Dad sang for someone to fly him to the moon,
to let him play among the stars, while Mom
held up the lighter to another Marlboro.

But when the doctor started speaking . . .

The tip of the Marlboro was a bright red star.
Her lips pursed and she released a ring of Saturn,
which dissolved as we caught at it, as my dad sang Mars.

When you realized what the doctor was saying . . .

They were closer to the storm in the front seat.
The high beams, weak as steam against the walled swirling,
only illuminated what we couldn't see.

When he described it, the tumor in the brain and what it meant . . .

See, we were children. Then we weren't. Or my brother wasn't.
He was driving now, he gripped the steering wheel
with both hands and stared hard at the panicked wipers.

What did you feel?

Just sleet, the slick road, the car going way too fast,
no brother beside me in the back seat, no singing father,
no mother, no ring of Saturn to catch at as it floats.

Scan

I wanted to watch the game.
The small room strewn

with magazines was too dark
to read in, lightless

but for the frenzied pulsing
of the muted screen

above the door, and for the
door, which a nurse would open

now and again onto
a blazing corridor

that this one's wife or that
one's son, when called, would leave for,

or drift back from, dazed
either way, coming

or going, by the light
first, then the dark.

I wanted to watch the game,
I could tell that time

was running out by how
the white team, spreading

the court, touch-passed
the ball from corner to key

to corner so quickly that
the yellow team couldn't

get close enough to foul,
the ball sailing just

beyond their reach as they lunged
for it, scrambled and dove,

frenetic, hopeless, in a
dumb-show of defeat.

I wanted to watch it, but
the lady next to me,

soon as my brother's name
was called, was telling me

"the story," what we all share,
our bond, our lingua franca,

the before, the after, signs
now unmistakable

but at the time ignored
until the stroke, or seizure.

I wanted to watch the game.
I wanted to tell the lady,

Lady, I don't know how long
my brother has to live,

my sister's dead, my parents
are dying, can't you just let

me watch the game in peace?
But the automatic iron

gears of courtesy
engaged, and I was just

so many different engines
of attention: a nameless friend,

a confessor, an innocent
who can't have any idea

of what it's like to live
with someone you've spent your life with

and see him this way, unable
to feel emotion, like a

well-trained zombie,
because that's what the tumor

damaged, where the feelings
come from in the brain.

My goodness, you must think
it's so selfish of me

to complain like this. I should
feel grateful, shouldn't I?

I mean, I know he has
no sense of what we're all

going through for him,
and so he can't really

love us now, not me, not
even the children. But at least

he isn't scared of dying
since he can't feel fear —

it's a blessing really . . .
She looked away and

smiled, apologizing
for going on like that,

the way my sister did
in her last days each time

the nurse would decompact
her bowels by hand — I'm

sorry, she'd mumble, barely
conscious, sorry, sorry,

till the nurse was through,
her relief, then, less relief

from pain than from the need,
even then, to think of

others. (Didn't we all say
it was so like Beth to do that?)

She could just sleep and
no longer fuel the still

inexorable autonomous
machinery of obligations

that displace us even as
they make us who we are.

Now he was back, her husband,
he smiled when she introduced me,

and before they left for the next
test, next waiting room,

he placed his hand on my shoulder
and said, Good luck, Godspeed,

said it as if he meant it,
as if he could feel it, the gesture

performing itself without him,
like a blinking eyelid

with no eye behind it.
Up on the screen, the crowd

stormed the court in silence
as time expired. My brother

was probably by then
inside a long white

tube where he'd doze while
pictures were being taken

of all the hidden places
in his brain. He was sealed off

and all open, he was free
and confined, and I wanted

him to stay there, where
he didn't have to apologize

to anyone for the delay,
the inconvenience, as

he would to me, as always,
when he returned. I wanted

to sit here and keep watching
the nodding, radiantly

bald head of the color
commentator as he smiled a stiff

smile and held the mike
up high toward the mouth

of the stooping six-ten player
of the game who (I could tell)

was thanking the good Lord
for his God-given this or that.

The Match

O Lord of life,
              bountiful
                      as sunlight
and like the sun
                  impartial
                        in your shining
neither kind nor unkind
                      though we call you both
at different moments
                    as you flash
                            refracted
through the ever-shifting
                        prism of what happens —
it's you yourself
                you give to
                        when you give
to us —
        yourself
                you show yourself to
                            through us
whenever we're on display
                        to one another —
you
    sorting us out
                    haphazardly
                          for the
selections
          we think are only
                      ours to make.

Who else but you
                    could have arranged the scene:
the two boys
                    in the hotel pool,
                                        the girl
at the pool's edge,
                    legs dangling in the water,
all three
            so freshly post-
                                pubescent that
the change itself
                    could have been happening
right then
            before us
                        when we stopped to watch,
my brother and I,
                    returning to his room
after a day of treatment.
                                We could tell
by how completely
                    they ignored her that
their every
            gesture
                        had the girl in mind,
hands locked
            around each other's necks,
                                        their fore-
heads touching,

water lights
                              and streams of water
running everywhere
                              along their arms,
backs, shoulders,
                              every trembling muscle,
                                             force
requiring counterforce
                              to feel how strong
it is, how irresistible,
                              as now
one quickly slipped down
                              under the other's arm
and groaning
                              lifted the twisting
                                             torso up
and threw him
                              and was on him
                                             before the splashes fell.

You neither kind nor unkind,
                              both the end
and means,
                              the contest and the prize,
                                             the girl
who dipped her calves, her
                              dripping fine-boned ankles
in and out

of the water

way too non-

chalantly

to be nonchalant,

and the boys

who grappled

in what could

have been the first

rush of the flowering

strength inside them

of you

who were no less

there

inside my brother,

no less ferociously

inside

each flowering cell

no medicine

could beat back or slow.

Angel of being,

Proteus,

who are

all your

disguises,

your many forms,

there is no blessing,

no secret to be

wrestled from you,
                              neither
kind nor unkind,
                    with magnificent indifference
sorting us out
                    to see who best
                              will serve
your riot of good fortune:
                              I had to hold
my brother's arm
                    to keep him steady
while the two boys and girl
                              began to swim
together
          in a circle
                    so we couldn't tell
who was chasing whom.
                              He said he was tired,
he wanted to get
                    back to his room
                              and sleep
before the sickness
                    came on
                              and he woke
entangled in the sheets,
                    drenched,
                              doubled up,
contorted,

shifting

    all through the long night

from side to side

    as if somehow

       to get

a better grip

    on what he wrestled with.

The Phone Call

The mangled speech, aphasic
pratfalls halfway through the
sentences, the voice
weak, tremulous, taken
by suffering so far
beyond what it once was
it's already otherworldly —
Heracles borne on his litter.

You can't imagine it.

Can't eat, can't drink, can't do a
thing except just lie
in bed before the TV
he's too sick to watch,
one ulcer running down
all the way from lip
to anus like a shirt
of fire burning inside out.

You can't know what it's like.

And even Ellen, sweet Ellen:
her transcendent body just
a torment to him now —
an unignorable
reminder of what he can't
be for her, won't ever be

again, though someone will.
Shirt of fire underneath the skin.

You can't imagine it at all.

What he wants to tell his children
when they call is don't,
you no longer have a father.
The slow annihilation
itself, each agonizing
moment of it now
an eternal labor —
alone on a high crag.

You can't. Don't even try to.

The Accident

While it was happening,
      the absolute
not me of it, the all
      of a sudden see-
through whir of wings beside me
      that the late sun
just as I looked up
      turned to a hovering
flash, a watery gray —
      green iridescence
as the beak dipped into
      a funnel of blossom,
dipped and was gone, and not even
      the blossom's white
tip bent in its going,
      or shivered —

While this, which could have happened
      without me, here
or elsewhere, happened the way
      it did, and would
continue happening
      for others, for no one,
for nothing but the blind urge
      of its happening,
this ever-transient
      accidental
crossing of momentums
      that was, in this case,

beautiful but could
        have not been and so
seemed all the more consoling
        for the thought —

even the thought of death,
        just then, consoling,
shaping itself inside me
        as the now there
now not there hovering
        of bird, flower, late
sun iridescences —
        beloved singers,
you who in the aftermath
        surged from the shadows
to sing in your different voices
        the same song, Route
of evanescence, Mother
        of beauty, It
avails not, time nor place,
        distance avails not,

if you had known, just then,
        three hundred miles
away, in another state,
        that one of the nurses
getting my brother up
        from the commode

and back to bed, the one
          who held him on
his left side, the dead side,
          all of a sudden
lost hold of him and, as
          he fell hard, grabbed
for the loose papery gown
          and ripped it off,
so that he lay there naked,
          utterly exposed —

beloved singers, tricksters
          of solace, if
you had known this, seen
          this, as I did not,
you would have offered him
          no sumptuous
destitution, no fire-
          fangled feathers,
or blab about death as being
          luckier than one
supposes. You would have bowed
          your heads, you would
have silently slipped back
          into the shadows
out of which you surged forth,
          singing to me.

Joy

What never comes when called.
      What hides when held.
Guest
  most at home where least
      expected. Vagrant
balm of Gilead.
    What, soon as here,
      becomes
the body's native ground and,
     soon as not,
its banishment.
    Coming and going,
      indifferent,
magisterial.
    My lovely daughter —
walking me to the car
     to say goodbye
the day I left
   to keep watch at my brother's
bedside —
    suddenly
     singing "I
feel pretty, oh so
    pretty"
     as she raised
her arms up in a loose oval
      over her head
and pirouetted all along the walk.

Savage
     and magisterial —
          the joy of it,
the animal candor of
       each arabesque,
each leaping turn and counterturn,
         her voice
now wobbly
     with laughter,
       "And I pity
any girl
    who isn't me
      tonight."
Savagely beautiful,
      not so much like
the lion that the camera
       freezes
        in mid-
pounce, claws
     outstretched for the stumbling
         antelope,
as like the herd
     escaping
      that the camera
pans to, zig-
    zagging,
      swerving as one,
their leaping strides now

          leaping higher,

                    faster,

even after,

      it seems,

          the fear subsides —

after the fear and

          the relief

             they keep

on running

      for nothing but

             the joy of running,

though

      it could be

          any one of them

is running

      from its fallen

            mother or father,

sister or brother,

        across the wide

             savanna,

under a bright sun

        into fresher grass.

Up Against

It was your game.
You invented it,
mastered it, played it
undefeatably against me
your little brother
in the evening all
throughout the summer
every summer up
till I was undefeatably
not little anymore.

Up Against, your front-stoop
baseball in which
(at least in memory)
I'm always in "the field,"
out on the street while you,
both batter and pitcher,
lean over the brick
steps, tennis ball
in hand, eye on the point
of the third step which
(if you can hurl the ball
just so against it) will send
the ball high over my head
into the front yard
of the house across from ours.

No joy like the joy
of that, the execution

better than the dream,
sensation of triumph so
extreme you didn't have
to rub it in, the blasé
look of feigned
bewilderment (Gee whiz,
did I do that?) itself
the measure of your exaltation,
and of your need as well
to keep me there so
you could go on playing—

for it was summer,
it would be hours yet
before we're called inside;
summer—and you have just
now made the ball hit
with a sweet whomp
against the brick that
sends it sailing up
and over your brother's out-
stretched hands; have seen,
more sweetly still,
the fury on his face,
the fury and despair.
By God it's summer and
you've cleared the bases.
There's no one out.
The inning could go on forever.

The Last Scene

Extravagant sweep
                of clear sky
                                darkening
in the big picture window
                           beside the bed,
lights here and there
                     already flashing all
across the city down below us —
                              Ellen
and the girls out somewhere,
                       you and I alone,
you with your eyes closed,
                     I with a drink in hand:
you suddenly in character,
                     your voice
a wraith's voice,
                faint, stumbling,
                         slurry
with morphine,
               and yet
                  still artful
                       as ever,
even if the art
            was obvious,
the dying brother
              playing the dying brother —
Do you think
           you have a problem

with that?

the question

masking a declaration,

the brother

a savior,

the savior a judge,

not all that different from

before except that now

the dying had

distilled

all doubt away

as you repeated,

Do you think

you have a

problem?

"Me? With what?"

I too in character now,

the character

without character,

the little brother who

in your mind proves

the truth

of all you think

by his resistance to it,

pulling

the scene off

by refusing to play it,

pretending not to know:

"With what?"
                  With that,
                                    head tilted to the shot
glass,
          "This?"
                    my one desire now
                                        a little shtick,
a final moment
                    of material —
                                        "This?
A problem?
                    Not at all.
                                        There's plenty more
where that came from,
                            almost a whole bottle."
You imperturbable,
                    Look at yourself,
how you sit here
                    drinking all alone.
                                        "Well, mea
gulpa.
          Are you happy now?"
                                    You drink
a lot.
          "I have a lot
                    to drink about."
And that was that.
                    For now you drifted off,

or seemed to,
　　　　　　　your eyes closed,
　　　　　　　　　　　　head turned away,
the two of us
　　　　　　together
　　　　　　　　　　for the last
time ever on the stage
　　　　　　　　　　of being brothers,
our see-through
　　　　　　　　figures in the picture window
spectral and vast
　　　　　　　　against the city
　　　　　　　　　　　　flashing
a ghostly circuitry
　　　　　　　of nerves
　　　　　　　　　　within
the ancient masks we wore,
　　　　　　　　　　the hand I lifted,
the drink I knocked back
　　　　　　　　　　in a final toast
in honor of the timing,
　　　　　　　　　the concentration
that neither
　　　　　　one of us
　　　　　　　　could ever break.

Fly

Eyes half closed
but flicking
urgently from
side to side
that last long day
as if in search
of some way
out of the dying
body that just
would not die,
as if the body
teased itself
with glimpses of
being rid
of body, the cruel
vision of it
there a moment
above the bed,
then not there, where
is it now? why
won't it keep still?

Eyes half closed,
spasmodic, frantic
as the fly
beside the bed,
the inexhaustible
faint banging
against the window

as it flitted from
side to side, a
tight little knot
of panic on
the glass that teased
it, tortured it,
being at once
the vision of what
the fly so
wanted to get
out into and
the very thing
that kept it
where it was.

The Big Screen

What did it mean, the moaning? Or could you even
call it a moan, what bore no trace of a voice
      we could recognize as his?
Was there even a his by then? Or was it only
a sound, mere sound of the body becoming a thing,
      a spasm, a mere electrical event?
And what about the good hand that, while he moaned,
would move slowly from time to time across
      his forehead, his clenched eyes, his nose —
was it to soothe himself? Did his head still hurt
despite the constant morphine? Or was the gesture
      itself habitual by then,
as automatic as a tic? And when
he wet the bed, and we had to get his shirt off
      and roll him side to side to slip
the clean pad underneath him — as he lay there naked,
what did it mean really when he began
      to sob those dry sobs, infant sobs,
sobs of Can't anyone stop this, can't anyone hear me?
Why won't you do something? And what, too, did
      the fist mean when it rose and shook
as if in protest, as if to say I don't deserve this,
I'll get you you asshole you fucking fuck God — look
      what you did to me! Is that what it was?
Or was it Give me back my body, or
Just get me out of it already, or,
      shivering as the fist shook,
could he have just been cold? And if he was,
was he, by then, even aware of it?

Maybe, as the four of us looked on,
trying to ease him any way we could,
maybe we all along were only sitting
    alone in the same theater in which
from four booths four projectors projected pictures
that were too weak to reach all the way to the screen,
    so that like yarns of light they got
all tangled up in the dark before us while
beyond their tangling ("I think he's . . ." "No,
    no, look, it's got to be . . .")—the screen
stayed blank, the screen of the moaning, the screen
of the dry sobs, of the shaking fist and clenched eyes—
    all of it blank, white, empty,
as if the theater were closed, the seats all upright,
the aisles swept clean, and the four of us somehow there
    too late and too early, before the previews,
after the feature presentation, our eyes
fixed on the big screen nothing flickered on.

Three Questions

What was it like to see him die?

I was thinking how the body,
    mine, not his,
didn't care
    about any of it —
not the hush
around the bedside, not
"the stillness in the air,"
not even my own sorrow —
    it just
went on blindly
    feeding on the food
I'd fed it
        till it
needed more, a furnace
craving fuel,
           and moved me
to the refrigerator
where I made myself
stare too long
at the refrigerator light
so when I looked
       away
the afterimage
    like a ghostly
pulse appeared
      to hover
  a moment in the air

before my eyes before it failed
        and there was nothing
between the food and me.

Was he ready to die?

In the last moment his eyes
        opened, and the blue
rims of the beautiful
                        pale green
irises
        looked toward us as he
all of a sudden rose
on some invisible wave and
        just as suddenly
sank back, and the eyes
stayed open like a doll's
eyes, wide, unblinking,
and the doll was
                        in a box inside
a closet in a house
        no one was living in.

Was he at peace?

Like the refrigerator light
after the door is closed.

Broadway Revival

What were my lines?
                    The spotlight on my face
made everything pitch-
                    black beyond the stage,
invisible.
        Encased in light, I was alone
and looked at.
            The air too thick with heat, too bright.

What were my lines?
                    The packed house held its breath.
Who was I playing?
                    And why were you there
                                    watching
from the wings,
            the script I somehow
                        knew you had
by heart
        splayed
                open in your palm,
one finger pointing
                to the very words
I couldn't
        for the life of me
                    remember?

Wasn't this your
                stage, your part,
                        your one

and only

       home, you liked to say, where speech
was song,

     and movement dance and

            you were most
at ease, a natural,

        most truly who
you were

     when you were someone else?

               Tell me,
I whispered through clenched

        teeth,

         tell me my lines.

And did the silence mean

        you were enjoying this?
Or were we both

     in being there that way
just following another

      script

        in which
my lines were

     these, and yours

        your silence,

           as if
the theater were itself a stage

        inside
a theater in which

I play
        the brother
who doesn't know his lines,
                and you the actor
who waits there in the wings,
                who holds the script,
who knows it all
        by heart and
                will not say.

If I Only Knew Then

Let's say you did. Let's
        say there was
a moment half a century ago,

three years before my birth, when you
        had only Beth
and David, and I was, in effect,

where they are now, though my time there,
        of course, would end;
let's say the vision came to you

on a winter night in that back room
        off the kitchen
of the old apartment that you remember

now as an inside pastoral
        retreat; on a night
like any other night in which

the baby's whimpering, his phlegmy
        mews and gurgles,
have awakened Beth, who calls out, Mommy,

Mommy, standing up in her crib,
        shaking the crib bars,
crying, when she sees you go

first to the baby, just as the baby
        too cries when you leave
him to go to Beth. Like every night

you're tired, impatient, angry,
        too indispensable
to stand it, just as you'll later be

unable to stand it when you're not;
        let's say it's then
before you say, Go to sleep already!

Will you just go to sleep, and leave them,
        letting them cry,
not picking them up as all the books say

you mustn't if nobody's sick,
        or wet, or hungry —
let's say it's then that it swoops down on you,

the certainty that you'd outlive them,
        that one would even
shun you at the end, the vision too

unbearable to believe, too vivid
        to ignore,
as if you were your own Cassandra,

lingering there a little longer,
　　　rubbing the girl's back,
wrapping the baby tighter in his blanket,

singing them back to sleep this one time
　　　in a voice less rushed
but still rushing not to get too far

off schedule with these darkening preludes
　　　about what happens
when the wind blows and the bough breaks.

The Old Man

The day after his son died
all that day
grief was the good mother
                              as he lay in silence
in the bed on his side
knees drawn to chest
hand under cheek
                    eyes open.
Grief was the womb
his posture presupposed;
the absoluteness of it,
                          the encircling
wash of *nothing*
worse than this
can ever happen
                    made it soothing,
peaceful — it seemed
his every feature
was being bathed
                    away until
his face was like a face
before the least
expression scathes it,
                        his eyes the eyes
before the eyelids form,
fish eyes that do not
need to close now
                    not to see.

To the Body

Mutable port of entry, port of call,
cargo and ship —
                        where can we go without you?
Where can we be?
                        Anarchic borderland
patrolled by piercing, tattoo, shawl, veil, collar,
earlock and dreadlock;
                        ventriloquist of genes,
vector of history,
                        the agonizing
                                        stage
on which the anorexic girl performs
clay dreaming spirit dreaming clay;
                                        at one
and the same
                        time pleasure dome
                                        and torture chamber,
prisoner and
                        cell and cell
                                        wall through which
the prisoner taps out
                        a message to
the prisoner in the
                        next cell who taps his message
back through the wall
                        that, separating,
                                        links.

Even the gods
                    and the dead are
                                        inconceivable
without you,
                    white-vested specter, "tenuous air" —
"But O as to
                    embrace me she inclined" —
O bosom of Abraham,
                              the whole world in his hands!
Propitiations
                    and provisions all
assume you:
                    wine jars, jewels, and
                                        honey cakes,
baubles and trinkets
                    in the Sun
                                        King's tomb,
my addle-brained Aunt Tilly saying,
                                        after
the funeral,
                    that she just couldn't let
them close the casket till
                    she'd placed a golf
ball in her husband's hand
                    because my Amos,
you know, he always had
                    such a thing
                                        for golf;

and yes I mocked her —

                    what did I know about you then? —

I whispered in my

           brother's ear,

                  Thank God

he didn't have a thing for cottage cheese.

       I mocked her and you took

                  your own

                        sweet time

to get revenge,

          nearly three decades later

when I saw

        how the embalmers had

                  slicked back

my brother's hair,

          and it wasn't

              him,

                it just

wasn't him, and I

       too

          wouldn't let

them close the casket

         till I'd tried to palm

the hair down

       over his forehead

           the way he kept it,

as if the frigid skin would

         somehow thereby

become less frigid if

                    I got it right.

Death's feedbag, mother lode

                         of yearning, salve

and sore:

            even the worst there is

                       to suffer

seems in my ignorance of it

                  to be no

less precious:

            and though it does no good to ask

you this,

        I ask it anyway:

                 keep me

and those I love

            with you in safety

                    for

a long time yet,

            steer clear of the hidden reef

you also are,

          who are

              at once the fire

eating the wood

            and the wood that,

                  burning,

          eats the fire.

Song and Dance

Did you ever have a family?

                         Dark
dining room,
            bright kitchen,
                       white steam
from the big pot my mother's stirring
reaching in wavy tendrils to her face,
around her face, all the way around
to me at the table, then beyond me
into the darkness where my brother is.

Were you ever a child?

                    I'm hungry
but I know we'll
           eat soon,
                      so
even the hunger's sweet.

Did you ever really have a brother?

                       He's singing
there in the dark
         corner
                  beside the stereo,
the volume turned down so low
all we hear is him, his voice, and
his eyes are closed so that there's
nothing around him anywhere
that might reveal he isn't
who the song insists he is.

And that is?
                    Irresistible,
unforgettable,
                    someone
                              to whom
as in imaginary gardens
where "the nectarine and curious
peach into my hands themselves
do reach," love comes as soon
as called, comes just as dreamed.

Did any of this ever happen?
                              The hunger's
sweet,
          it's as if
                    the song weaves
through the fragrance of the braiding
steam from him to me to her
to me to him because her eyes
are closed now too; her
slippered feet tap, caper
a soft shoe while the ladle
sways in her hand as she stirs.

Were you ever a child?
                              I know
I'll eat soon.
                    Did you ever really have a brother?
You should have

heard him,

his voice was

unforgettable, irresistible, his voice
was an imaginary garden
woven through with fragrance.

Did you ever have a family?

Their eyes are closed.

That's how I know

we're there

inside it,

it's made of sound and steam
that weaves between dark
dining room, bright kitchen.
We're there because I'm hungry,
and we'll all be eating soon
together, and the hunger's sweet.

Last Impressions

When the doctor asked you, "If we deem it necessary to perform the surgery, will you be able to afford the operation?" you held up one talmudic finger à la Jackie Mason as you answered, "And if I can't afford the operation, will you deem it necessary to perform the surgery?"

And after the surgery, the Groucho Marx you whispered in my ear when the neurosurgeon, grim as an accountant, though without the personality, presented the two paths of treatment you could take — do nothing and live pretty well (little or no "premorbidity" is how he put it) until the end or go the standard route of chemo/radiation and be very sick but increase the odds of living more than a year from zero to one percent — your voice so perfect I could smell the smoke from the invisible cigar you held between two fingers as you whispered, "It's like having to choose your favorite Menendez brother."

On the eve of your second surgery, your invention of the James Brown Alarm Clock that goes off, shouting, "Help me now! Help me! Help me!"

The Jimmy Cagney you reserved exclusively for the examination room, where the two of us would wait sometimes for hours for the doctor to arrive with the MRI results; you pacing in that room that was hardly bigger than a closet, agitated, cursing, unreachable inside your mounting panic, and when you finally had had enough and opened the door and stood there in the doorway looking out at the doctors, nurses, patients bustling to and fro, you'd catch a nurse's eye and suddenly Cagney, holding on to imaginary prison bars, would ask, "Any news from the governor?"

The freakish taffy of your face doing Crazy Guggenheim whenever my kids would call, the lower jaw askew, the mouth wrenched sideways, only the corner of it moving as the exuberant dumb voice says, "Hiya Joe, hiya Mista Dunahee-hee-hee."

Or later, toward the end, your Bette Davis, when the nurse would ask you every morning how the paralyzed left arm was doing: "Dead," you'd say, the right hand lifting up the left, the furtive breathiness between the *d*'s just right, the nurse who knew what to expect by then still cracking up when you say it twice more, "Dead. Dead," before you let the hand go and it falls like someone else's hand back to the bed.

Comedy, from the Greek *komoidia,* out of *komoidos* — *komos* meaning revel, and *oidos,* singer. The comic, then, is the singer in the revels.

So if your cancer was the gravity that pulled you every moment down into the isolating black hole of your dying, could the impressions, comebacks, quips, the little shuffle-off-to-Buffaloes you'd do for the nurses after each examination, even after the last one — two days later you'd be paralyzed — could all that comedy have been the grace that kept you here among us where you could go on being the comedian, the singer in the revels, joking as if your life depended on it?

58

But where's the rage in that? The rage that ran through all the voices, all the manic shtick, the refusal not to be funny — "Death, where is thy sting-a-ling?" — as if the cancer wanted all the jokes to end, as if the cancer weren't a random spin of the genetic wheel, a biochemical mishap run amuck, absurd for its impersonality, but a character from Central Casting, Uriah Heep or Scrooge, or worse in your pantheon of villains, a puckerbutted Pooh-Bah in a white tuxedo on a busy corner hailing a cab, and your Jerry Lewis's "LAAAADY" or your Arnold Schwarzenegger's "Dis is not a tuma!" is the cab that doesn't stop but roars by through a puddle that sprays the immaculate white suit black with muck?